THE MOTIVATION POCKETBOOK

D0645906

By Max A. Eggert BSc, MA, FCIPD, CFAHRI, ABPS, MAPS

Drawings by Phil Hailstone

"One of the best I have seen on the complex subject of motivation. Max has managed to integrate and synthesise a plethora of data into a compact, concise and very readable form. Good reading."

Tony Grant-Salmon, Managing Director, Knowles Europe.

To the late great Hugh S. Knowles who not only knew all this stuff but was humble enough to put it into practice.

Special thanks to Caitlyn Barnier who created the WP version from both poor spelling and handwriting.

Published by:
Management Pocketbooks Ltd
Laurel House, Station Approach, Alresford, Hants SO24 9JH, U.K.
Tel: +44 (0)1962 735573   Fax: +44 (0)1962 733637
E-mail: sales@pocketbook.co.uk
Website: www.pocketbook.co.uk

This edition published 1999. Reprinted 2000, 2001, 2003, 2005, 2006.

© Max A. Eggert 1999

ISBN-13   978 1 870471 60 2
ISBN-10   1 870471 60 1

British Library Cataloguing-in-Publication Data – A catalogue record for this book
is available from the British Library.

Design, typesetting and graphics by **efex ltd**.   Printed in U.K.

CONTENTS

Author's Introduction

Motivation is rather like a jellyfish. Everyone knows what it is but it is difficult to describe or define.

Consequently, motivation has given psychologists some real problems. If you cannot see or feel it, it becomes difficult to measure; if you can't measure it in some way, how do you know you have found it?

In an absolute sense motivation per se does not exist - it can only be inferred by looking at behaviour, quantifying changes in behaviour or by inviting individuals to talk about their needs or goals and why they do what they do.

Behaviour can be prompted by a whole host of things and the same motivational drives can produce all sorts of different behaviours. So you need to do more than just look at changes in behaviour or performance to understand motivation.

In spite of all these difficulties, the concept of motivation has proved very resilient, if not as rigorous as one would like. It continues to be useful as a management tool for understanding and for helping individuals, from the most senior to the most junior, give of their best at work.

Max Eggert
Bondi Beach, Australia
November 1998

1NTRODUCTION

HOW TO USE THIS BOOK

Since people are so complicated there is no one way of motivating them. To answer the question: 'How do I motivate Joe or Jenny?' one can only say: 'It all depends'.

It depends on:
- Joe or Jenny
- Their personality
- Their needs
- The type of work they do
- Their situation
- The urgency

and many, many other factors.

Consequently, there is no one simple theory that will assist you - no 'one size fits all' facility when it comes to motivation.

Even in a book of this size we mention lots of theories, not because they exist but because each one will help you in a particular given situation. Just as one man's meat is another's poison, so one person's motivation is another's procrastination!

HOW TO USE THIS BOOK

Use the following as a guide:

Problem		Motivation Theory	Page
When money does not motivate	→	Hierarchy Theory (Pyramid Man)	11
When people complain a lot	→	ERG Theory (Three Level Man)	19
When you can't give money	→	Token Theory (Token Man)	39
When there is a lack of direction	→	Goal Theory (Soccer Man)	41
When people work in teams	→	Group Theory (Social Man)	47
How to motivate professionals	→	Two Factor Theory (Growth Man)	49
When work is boring	→	Two Factor Theory (Growth Man)	49
When rewards are not working	→	Expectancy Theory (Expectant Man)	58
When managing a culture change	→	Expectancy Theory (Expectant Man)	58
When your managers are poor	→	X & Y Theory (Good Man/Bad Man)	72
When you have a difficult person	→	People Types	77

HOW TO USE THIS BOOK

However, always remember the basic
rule of management:

**If what you do does not work,
do something different!**

When motivating people you have to be like a
detective who wants to get into a suspect's
house: you use lots of different picks to create
the right key for the lock.
When you begin you do not know which of the
little picks is going to be required, so you just keep
trying until you unlock the door, or in this case the
person. Everyone has a motivational lock; this book
gives you the theories and hints on which keys to use
and how to turn them to your advantage.

SO MANY THEORIES

Why are there so many different theories about motivation? Because:

- Motivation is an artificial construct so there is no comprehensive way of examining it
- An individual goal can be reached in any number of different ways - or motivations
- A single goal can satisfy a whole host of different needs - and thus motivations
- People are different in their needs - and thus their motivations are different
- Individuals frequently change their aspirations and their needs - and consequently their motivation differs in each situation

Different theories have been developed to account for different aspects of the concept of motivation.

INTRODUCTION

THE SEED ANALOGY

YOU CANNOT MOTIVATE ANY ONE

You cannot make a seed grow, but you can provide the right conditions for it to develop into its full potential.

This book helps you understand and use the motivational theories and approaches to help people grow and give of their best.

BUT YOU CAN PROVIDE THE ENVIRONMENT IN WHICH THEY GROW

ASSUMPTIONS

Because there is no one theory of motivation the first part of this book, which covers the main theories, is divided into one large section covering need theories, followed by two smaller sections for process theory and for dispositional theories (Types, Disposition & Personality).

The main assumptions each type of theory makes are as follows:

1. Need theories
- All employees are alike
- All situations are alike
- There is 'One Best Way'

2. Process and dispositional theories
- Behaviour is determined by a combination of factors
- People make decisions about their own behaviour in organisations
- Different people have different types of needs, desires and goals
- People decide between alternative plans of behaviour based upon their perceptions (expectancies) of the degree to which a given behaviour will lead to a desired outcome

3. Dispositional theories
- People are different
- Different people have different needs
- Personality has an effect on motivation

NEED THEORIES

THE BASIC MODEL

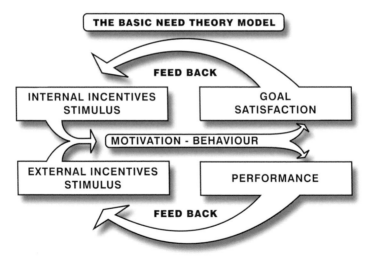

THE BASIC NEED THEORY MODEL

FEED BACK

| INTERNAL INCENTIVES STIMULUS | GOAL SATISFACTION |

MOTIVATION - BEHAVIOUR

| EXTERNAL INCENTIVES STIMULUS | PERFORMANCE |

FEED BACK

NEED THEORIES

PYRAMID MAN

THE HIERARCHY OF NEEDS

The 'hierarchy of needs' theory is based on the premise that individuals require satisfaction on ascending levels of need.

Maslow, who developed the theory, suggested that when one level of satisfaction is achieved another level of need becomes important, rather like an ascending staircase.

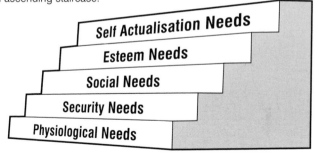

PYRAMID MAN

THE HIERARCHY OF NEEDS

Sometimes it is shown
as a pyramid.

Self Actualisation

Esteem

Social

Security

Physiological

We explain each level of need.

NEED THEORIES

PYRAMID MAN

1. Physiological needs

The most basic needs, at the foot of the pyramid, are physiological, namely:

- Air
- Water
- Food
- Sleep
- Sex

These are essential for the continuation of life. If they were removed our lives would be endangered. Some would even fight to secure them. At the most basic level we will work for food and drink.

Once this physiological need is satisfied we move up to the second level, the need for security.

2. Security needs

Here we need to be safe from harm and to achieve this we require:

- Shelter and clothing
- Personal safety and security

Once this security need is satisfied we move up to the third level which represents our social needs.

PYRAMID MAN

3. Social needs

Since we are not social islands we need:
- Friends and colleagues
- To be part of a group
- To be part of a team

We want people to talk to, who will share our joys and concerns, our hopes, fears and aspirations. We want to be part of a team and experience group solidarity.

Once this social need has been satisfied we move up to the fourth level which is our need for esteem.

PYRAMID MAN

4. Esteem needs

This is about enjoying a personal status. Within our group or team we need status and a role to give us individuality and an identity. This allows us to be ourselves and express our personality. We are part of the group, but we also enjoy a particular role and maintain individual and personal status.

Once this need is satisfied we move up to the fifth and final need, which enjoys the complicated name of self actualisation.

5. Self actualisation needs

This is our need to be the best that we can be, with all the talents and gifts that we have. It is about being our true selves: having achieved all that we have set ourselves out to achieve, being what we want to be, feeling satisfied with our position and knowing that we have done the very best we can with what we have.

PYRAMID MAN

MANAGEMENT TIPS

Physiological needs

- Ensure that remuneration is at least sufficient to pay for the very basic necessities of life such as food, drink, clothing and rent. In addition, make sure there are adequate breaks, holidays and time for employees to rest and recuperate.

Security needs

- Ensure the working environment is safe
- Provide safety equipment, protective clothing to ensure safe working practices when employees work in potentially dangerous environments
- Provide safe working tools and equipment
- Provide lockers for individuals to keep their personal belongings secure

PYRAMID MAN

MANAGEMENT TIPS

Social needs

- Encourage individuals to form groups and teams by:
    - Allowing the same people to work together on a regular basis
    - Having similar job title groupings so that people can identify with each other
    - Wearing the same or similar uniforms
    - Encouraging the same people taking breaks together to facilitate social interaction and bonding
    - Making sure that people can interact with each other during work
    - Allowing groups to differentiate themselves from other groups
    - Having regular briefing meetings so that people can identify with each other through the information they receive
    - Having team safety meetings to discuss common concerns
    - Having team production meetings where all are involved and can make a contribution

NEED THEORIES

PYRAMID MAN

MANAGEMENT TIPS

Esteem needs

● Encourage individuals and reward their personal contribution and achievements by such things as:

- Employee of the month
- Individual bonuses
- Name tags on uniforms
- The right to decorate and personalise their own work space or area
- Long service awards
- Special service awards

- An active promotion-from-within scheme
- Self development programmes
- Personal responsibility for quality
- Personal responsibility for setting production targets
- Category of benefits rather than set systems with same for all

Self actualisation needs

Here individuals need to be able to visualise themselves being the very best they can. This can be affirmed by continually recognising good work, so that individuals think about themselves as doing a good job, and being great in their own way.

NEED THEORIES

THREE LEVEL MAN
ERG THEORY

In this theory there are only three levels of need: existence (E), relatedness (R) and growth (G).

Existence needs - Those things required to exist and survive, ie: the physiological and safety needs of a material nature - food, water, shelter (the first two levels of Maslow's Hierarchy)

Relatedness needs - Those things concerned with relationships and with the social structure, ie: being loved, needed and recognised (the third and fourth levels of Maslow's Hierarchy)

Growth needs - Those things to do with personal development and growth, ie: esteem and self actualisation. The difference from Maslow's theory is that dissatisfaction in a higher need can be compensated by a desire for the next need down the hierarchy. This increases the importance of the lower level need. Thus, a low 'growth' job could be compensated by more pay, or a low status job by better job security.

Note that when an employee complains, it may indicate dissatisfaction with a higher need and not the one complained of. A lot of effort, according to this theory, could wrongly be spent addressing the 'vocalised' problem and not the 'real' problem.

NEED THEORIES

THREE LEVEL MAN

SATISFACTION & REGRESSION PATHS

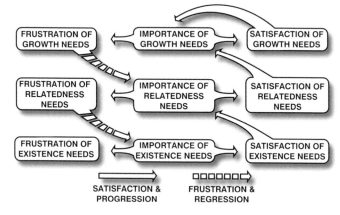

20 Note how the frustration of a higher need increases the importance of a lower need.

RAT MAN
BEHAVIOURIST THEORY

Behaviourist Theory is called Rat Man because Skinner, perhaps the most famous of all the behaviourist psychologists, did much of his work on rats.

This theory suggests that employees are motivated by what happens to them after they work at a particular task. What is the result of their work? Are they rewarded, punished or ignored?

The basics of this behaviourist theory are:

- It focuses on behaviour that can be seen and measured

- It suggests that all behaviour is learnt

- It suggests that behaviour is strengthened or diminished depending on the consequences of earlier behaviour

The theory can be shown diagrammatically as follows.

RAT MAN

SUMMARY OF CONSEQUENCES

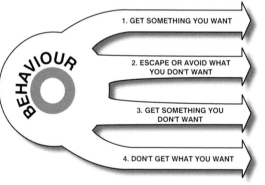

BEHAVIOUR

1. GET SOMETHING YOU WANT

2. ESCAPE OR AVOID WHAT YOU DON'T WANT

3. GET SOMETHING YOU DON'T WANT

4. DON'T GET WHAT YOU WANT

1. Positive reinforcement **R+** improves performance

2. Negative reinforcement **R-** improves performance

3. Punishment **P+** decreases performance

4. Extinction **P-** decreases performance

Usually in management we spend more time encouraging behaviour than rewarding it.

NEED THEORIES

RAT MAN

REWARDS AND REINFORCERS

The theory suggests something positive **R+** should occur after the desired performance (or behaviour). Consequently, rewards should be:

- Given after the desired behaviour
- Provided as soon as possible
- Personal in impact
- Valued by the recipient
- Delivered consistently
- Predictable by the recipient

RAT MAN

25 TIPS FOR NON-FINANCIAL RECOGNITION

Managers often feel that if they cannot give a financial reward they cannot motivate (shades of theory X see page 72). Remember, if people only worked for money they probably would not be working for your firm in the first place!

1. Smile
2. Thank you
3. Time off
4. Interesting project
5. A course/programme
6. A meal out
7. A card
8. A letter
9. An award
10. A badge/pin/tie
11. Book
12. Chocolates
13. Theatre/film tickets
14. Compliments
15. Positive feedback on performance
16. Invitation to coffee or lunch
17. Solicitations for advice
18. Recognition in a company publication
19. Job with more responsibilities
20. Visit to a supplier or customer
21. Extended breaks
22. Work on a personal project
23. Use of any equipment/machinery
24. Offer to make a presentation at a meeting
25. Offer to attend a conference/seminar

RAT MAN

PUNISHMENT NOT SO EFFECTIVE

As you can see from the model on page 22, if you were expecting punishment, the avoidance of it can be rewarding . However, wise managers will not, unless absolutely necessary, employ punishment because:

- It only produces a temporary reduction in the unacceptable behaviour
- It requires the constant presence of the punisher; the boss always has to be present
- It does not teach new or more appropriate behaviour
- It produces increased fear in the recipient which makes individuals less effective at work
- It produces emotional side-effects that transfer to others who are like the punisher (ie: other managers)
- It produces rigid and inflexible behaviour patterns
- It suppresses more behaviour than that which is punished
- It can result in counter-aggression and attempts to counter-control
- It is passed on down the line (ie: to fellow group members or subordinates)

NEED THEORIES

RAT MAN

MANAGEMENT TIPS

- Identify the specific behaviour and performance criteria that you require from the individual in the work place

- Measure how often the behaviour that you want occurs; this becomes a base line so you can subsequently measure any increase or decrease in that behaviour

- Identify what happens before and after the behaviour to provide clues as to what you might want to change

- Implement the reward or punishment required (punishment is usually less successful than a reward system)

- Measure the results in terms of changes in the behaviour of the individual; if it is positive continue with the reward schedule that you have instituted

MOTIVATION RULE 1

WHAT GETS ASKED FOR GETS DONE

**WHAT GETS MEASURED
GETS DONE BETTER**

**WHAT GETS REWARDED GETS DONE
BEST OF ALL**

People do what they do because of what happens to them when they do it.

MOTIVATION RULE 1

WHAT GETS ASKED FOR GETS DONE

Certain adverts for athletic footwear can say

but this is not good enough. Employees need to know in detail what is required of them. Poorly motivated employees need full instructions with the following components:

- Who is to do the work
- What needs to be done
- Why it needs to be done
- When it needs to be done by

- What resources to use
- What will happen if the work is not done
  - to other work
  - to the non-performer

Finish the instruction with the assumptive 'Thank you'.

After the employee has performed the required task, ensure that feedback, either positive or negative, is given.

MOTIVATION RULE 1

WHAT GETS ASKED FOR GETS DONE

Management example of an instruction

"Peter, I need that report by 5.00 pm tomorrow so that I can consolidate your figures into mine. We won't look good if our consolidated reports are not handed in on time. If you want somewhere quiet to work you can use the spare office.
I know you won't let me down -
thank you, Peter."

What gets rewarded gets
done best of all!

MOTIVATION RULE 1
WHAT GETS MEASURED GETS DONE BETTER

End results need to be specific and quantifiable.

Statements like 'work harder', 'do better' and 'you must improve your work' are NOT motivational, because they do not communicate to the individual exactly what is required from them.

Motivational instructions are always **SMART** that is:

>**S** pecific
>**M** easurable
>**A** greed
>**R** ealistic
>**T** ime bound

Qualification of a performance requirement is also helpful to the employee who then knows exactly what is expected of him or her. SMART instructions also ensure that the employee knows when the job has been completed, and this in itself is also motivational.

MOTIVATION RULE 1

WHAT GETS REWARDED GETS DONE BEST OF ALL

Employees need to be rewarded for good performance, otherwise they will not perform in the future.

When giving rewards aim to make them as specific as possible. In this way the employee knows exactly what has been done and why a reward is being given.

Example:

"Peter, thanks for letting me have that report on time. It meant I could do my consolidation in good time, too. Thanks, I really appreciate it."

MOTIVATION RULE 2

WHAT PEOPLE DO DURING THE WORKING DAY IS WHAT IS BEING REINFORCED BY THEIR MANAGERS

If people behave according to the rewards they receive, then what they do at work is a reflection of the current rewards individuals are receiving.

MOTIVATION RULE 2
MANAGEMENT TIPS

Given a free choice people will do what they like first, then what they next like and so on, through to what they don't like doing. Thus they leave their worst task till last. The employee uses a 'best the first' principle.

THE BEST FIRST
When employees apply the 'best the first' principle to their work then each time they complete a task the next job is less palatable. Their motivation for completing the next task is reduced.

If you reverse the process, the jobs as they get completed continually get better for the employee. So the smart manager will apply the principle of:

THE WORST FIRST
and
THE BEST LAST

A further refinement of this is what could be called 'Mother's Rule'.

MOTIVATION RULE 2

MANAGEMENT TIPS

Mother's Rule

This couples something not valued
with something that is valued
(since most kids prefer sweets
to vegetables).

*When you have
eaten your greens
you can have
your pudding*

To apply Mother's Rule to management and motivation, you combine what employees
don't like doing with something which they like very much, thus:

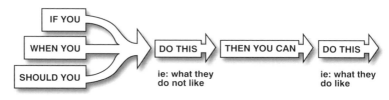

IF YOU
WHEN YOU
SHOULD YOU

DO THIS
ie: what they
do not like

THEN YOU CAN

DO THIS
ie: what they
do like

MOTIVATION RULE 3

IF PERFORMANCE IS NOT IMPROVING REINFORCEMENT IS NOT OCCURRING

If people behave according to the rewards they are receiving, then if there is no change in the behaviour (ie: performance), the rewards are not being changed enough to change the behaviour.

Keep changing the rewards until the behaviour of the employee changes in the direction that you want.

MOTIVATION RULE 3

MANAGEMENT TIPS

- Do not reward all employees equally if they do not all work equally hard - reward needs to be based on performance; if everyone is rewarded equally for unequal effort it will only encourage poor and average performance and will demotivate high performers

- Individuals need to know what they have to do to get a specific reward, so continue to tell them

- Be consistent in your rewards so that employees can predict outcomes

- If you must punish then do it in private - if it is public then good performers may resent you and thus reduce their motivation

- Honest and factual feedback, both positive and negative, is necessary for performance improvement

 *You cannot **not** communicate to employees - if you fail to recognise good performance and say nothing this will reduce effort in the employee.*

PLEASURE MAN
THE EFFECT THEORY

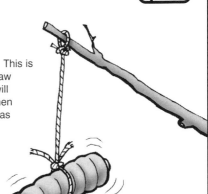

This is an early form of behaviourist theory.

People tend to maximise pleasure and avoid pain. This is what a psychologist named Thondike called 'The law of effect'. If what you do is pleasurable then you will do it more often. If your behaviour leads to pain then you are less likely to repeat that behaviour. This was further refined by another psychologist, Hull, who suggested that behaviour will become fixed when:

- Pleasure or pain come quickly after the behaviour

- This result of pain or pleasure is repeated frequently

- The pleasure or pain is significant for the recipient

NEED THEORIES

PLEASURE MAN

MANAGEMENT TIPS

- When employee behaviour is appropriate (ie: performed correctly) make the reward as specific as possible
- Ensure that pleasure (ie: the reward) is given as soon as possible after acceptable behaviour has occurred
- Disregard unacceptable behaviour unless there is a safety implication or something equally serious
- Continue to reward the behaviour once it has been learned
- Once the behaviour has been established the rewards can be gradually discontinued

TOKEN MAN

T.A. THEORY

Transactional Analysis, a theory developed by a therapist called Eric Berne, is a further variation on behaviourist theory. Berne suggested that one of the most basic and strongest motivating forces for the individual was to be positively recognised; to receive personal recognition from another human being. In Berne's language, individuals need 'strokes' from others to be emotionally and psychologically fulfilled. 'Strokes' can be anything from positive words through to a full personal commitment from another. From a casual statement like 'great job' to the very intimate statement 'I love you'.

So powerful is this need that, if positive strokes are not given, the stroke-hungry individual will be deliberately difficult and annoying just to receive some form of response. Even a negative stroke is better than being ignored and not receiving any strokes at all.

As in other reward systems, strokes have to be individualised and valued by the recipient to motivate certain types of behaviour: 'Different strokes for different folks'.

TOKEN MAN

MANAGEMENT TIPS

Managers should ask themselves:

- Am I giving enough positive strokes during the day to my subordinates?
- Are the strokes that I am giving valued by the individual employee, ie: does the recipient regard them as positive?
- When I express my disappointment at an employee's behaviour, can I be sure that he/she is not misbehaving just to get my attention (strokes)?
- How can I be sure that employees are not playing 'games' with me to ensure that they are getting enough strokes from me?

Verbal recognition is a great way of giving strokes, and is often overlooked by managers.

See 100 ways of saying well done on page 96.

NEED THEORIES

SOCCER MAN

GOAL THEORIES

Achieving goals is a motivating force in itself. Most individuals enjoy the satisfaction of working towards, and achieving, specific goals.

When an individual has set clear goals, performance will usually improve because:

- The employee orientates himself or herself to what is required
- The employee exerts effort to achieve the goal
- Task persistence is increased
- Ways of achieving the goal are pursued

Two further factors are relevant:

- The harder the goal is to achieve, usually the more effort is given to the task
- The more important the goal (in the individual's perception) the more effort is given to the task

It is important to gain agreement and acceptance of the goal by the employee. If the employee thinks the goal too difficult or unimportant he or she will not be motivated to perform.

SOCCER MAN

TYPES OF GOALS

There is a great variety of goals that the manager can set for a subordinate. Here are some of them:

Subjective Goals	Eg: doing the best you can, enjoying life more, being more successful
General Goals	Eg: winning, being the best, getting the appointment
Specific Goals	Behavioural targets that can be quantified
Outcome Goals	Focus on results and standards
Performance Goals	Emphasis on improvements to individual's previous performance
Process Goals	Concentration on what the individual must do to achieve the desired outcome

Understanding different types of goals is important because research suggests that certain types of goals are more conducive to changing behaviour.

SOCCER MAN
WHY DO GOALS WORK?

- Goals direct the individual's attention and activity towards the task
- Goals help individuals to direct effort towards achievement
- Goals help build the persistence required for achievement
- Goals encourage new learning strategies to ensure achievement
- Goals that are more specific are more achievable than generalised goals (eg: to be the best, or to be good)
- Goals are within the individual's control and thus are flexible
- Goals set more realistic expectations resulting in less anxiety and more motivation, and thus enhanced performance

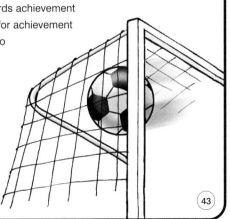

(43)

SOCCER MAN
GOAL SETTING GUIDELINES

Goals should be:

- Specific, measurable, behavioural
- Challenging but realistic

Explicit goals are far superior to general non-specific goals, such as 'must do better'.

The more difficult the goal the better the performance. But unrealistic goals, beyond the individual's ability, lead to frustration and failure. Consequently, goals must be difficult enough to challenge, but realistic enough to be possible.

Set small goals within the overall goal to see if immediate improvements occur. If they do, increase the performance criteria slowly, rather like a staircase - getting to the ultimate goal one step at a time.

NEED THEORIES

SOCCER MAN

THE ADVANTAGE OF SETTING GOALS

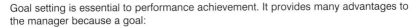

Goal setting is essential to performance achievement. It provides many advantages to the manager because a goal:

- Describes exactly what needs to be done
- Can encourage discussion and, therefore, personal ownership of and responsibility for what needs to be done
- Gives immediate feedback - either it is done or not
- Provides personal satisfaction when it is achieved
- Minimizes the possibility of drifting off target
- Concentrates the mind, providing the focus required for achievement

SOCCER MAN
TIPS FOR GOAL SETTING

- Specific performance goals must be identified which are quantifiable

- Employees need to understand why the goal is important and how it fits into the overall scheme of things

- Where possible, the employees should be involved in the process of goal setting so that, together with management, they own and support the goal

- Management must provide, as quickly as possible, measurable/quantifiable information/feedback on the progress towards the goal

- Feedback on progress towards the goal should be easy to understand and in an acceptable form for employees

SOCIAL MAN
GROUP THEORY

Way back in the 1920s it was discovered that if you treated people as special in themselves their performance improved.

Researchers were hard at work trying to discover the ideal environment for production employees, in terms of lighting, rest periods, benefits and physical comfort. What they discovered was that no matter what you did, as long as you treated people as special, their production would go up.

This became known as the Hawthorne Effect, because it was discovered at the Hawthorne plant of Western Electric in Chicago, Illinois.

The same researchers also discovered that groups have a tendency to set their own production norms, and ensure that new members of the group perform to the group norm. To do this, the group will use a variety of social mechanisms to ensure that new members do not either over-produce or under-produce.

NEED THEORIES

SOCIAL MAN
MANAGEMENT TIPS

- Where work allows, encourage the formation of natural working groups who see themselves as teams

- Recognise the teams that you have and make them feel special

- Regularly recognise and celebrate the contribution of the team to the overall success of the enterprise

- Encourage teams by setting challenging and appropriate performance goals

- Ensure that new employees are trained to company standards during induction, rather than letting established employees or the work group set the standards for the newcomers

GROWTH MAN

TWO FACTOR THEORY

The two factor theory of motivation states that satisfaction and dissatisfaction are two separate vectors, rather than at opposite ends of the same continuum. This suggests that certain specific things are required for motivation to take place. Some can prevent dissatisfaction but cannot, in themselves, bring satisfaction.

Single factor theory

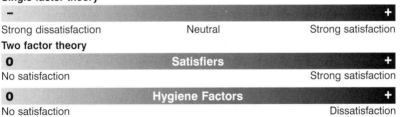

−		+
Strong dissatisfaction	Neutral	Strong satisfaction

Two factor theory

0	**Satisfiers**	**+**
No satisfaction		Strong satisfaction

0	**Hygiene Factors**	**+**
No satisfaction		Dissatisfaction

Things that prevent dissatisfaction but cannot bring satisfaction are called: **Hygiene Factors.**
Things that bring about job satisfaction are called: **Satisfiers.**

NEED THEORIES

GROWTH MAN

SATISFIERS AND HYGIENE FACTORS

SATISFIERS ➤
- Interesting work
- Challenging work
- Opportunities for achievement
- Recognition
- Advancement

HYGIENE FACTORS ➤
- Pay
- Supervision
- Working conditions
- Job Security
- Status

You can see how this links to the hierarchy theory of Maslow (page 11) because the hygiene factors relate closely to the more basic needs in the hierarchy.

GROWTH MAN

MANAGEMENT TIPS

Those aspects of a job which are necessary to satisfy the more basic requirements and biological drives of an employee, like adequate pay and conditions, must at least be present for an employee not to be dissatisfied.

The theory suggests that the hygiene factors must be present, rather like a base to provide a platform satisfaction, but they will not in themselves give job satisfaction or be motivators. For motivation and job satisfaction to occur, employees need the presence of the satisfiers: interesting work, challenge, etc.

Through this job enrichment employees 'grow' and are thus inspired to make a more significant contribution.

GROWTH MAN

JOB ENRICHMENT: THE MODEL

Following on from the two factor theory, it is assumed that satisfied employees are more motivated and thus their performance improves. A simple model would be:

EMPLOYEE SATISFACTION	EMPLOYEE MOTIVATION	EMPLOYEE PERFORMANCE
INCREASED	*INCREASED*	*INCREASED*

To provide job enrichment (and thus employee satisfaction) three major approaches can be used:

- Job enlargement
- Autonomous working groups
- Job rotation

NEED THEORIES

GROWTH MAN

JOB ENRICHMENT

Job enlargement

Look for anything which the employees can reasonably take on, such as:

- Personal quality control
- Material requisitioning
- Basic fault finding and correction
- Rota allocation

This enlarges the job and gives them more responsibility. They will, in turn, enjoy more satisfaction and thus become more motivated.

Autonomous working groups

When employees come together to work on a product or project, they can take over responsibility for the method of work planning and quality of what they do. In this way, satisfiers come into play increasing motivation and, consequently, productivity.

GROWTH MAN

JOB ENRICHMENT

Job rotation

This is used instead of employees endlessly repeating one single short cycle job.
For a whole shift employees are allowed as much variety in their task as possible,
moving from job to job. It is far more motivating to do six different jobs in a day than
to do the same one all the time.

Motivation is increased when teams of employees can work out and agree for themselves
who does what, when and for how long to achieve the agreed production targets.

NEED THEORIES

GROWTH MAN

THE 7 PRINCIPLES OF JOB ENRICHMENT

1 Minimum controls by management.

2 Maximum personal accountability for work for the individual.

3 Work should be in complete entities, ie: not just a small part of a whole.

4 Employees, where possible, should have control over which of the required tasks they undertake and when.

5 Easily understood feedback on performance and quality supplied direct to the employee.

6 Opportunity given to do new jobs according to ability and performance.

7 Individuals able to choose and arrange their jobs with the rest of their team.

SUMMARY OF MANAGEMENT TIPS

- All employees need to understand the relationship between how hard they have to work and the particular levels of performance they need to achieve
- Employees should have the ability and the confidence to achieve the outputs required
- Minimum controls should be placed on employees
- Key results should be expressed in **SMART** terms
- Employees should participate in setting output levels
- Feedback should be frequent, specific and understandable
- Employees need to be praised for good performance
- Employees should perceive pay as equitable
- Rewards given should be valued by employees
- Employees prefer to work in a production-orientated culture
- Employees should have jobs which maximise:
  - variety
  - significance of the work
  - the end product or service
  - personal autonomy
  - feedback on performance
  - possibilities for personal development
- Employees need to have an opportunity to discuss and comment on changes that affect them at and in work.

56

PROCESS THEORY

PROCESS THEORY

EXPECTANT MAN

LAWLER'S THEORY

The expectancy theory of motivation gives prominence to anticipated responses and outcomes. Lawler's theory is a variation of this.

Managers direct employees toward future rewards rather than past learning. Recognising the perceived effort/reward probability, employees work harder, performance is improved and rewards are given. This, in turn, brings satisfaction which further encourages effort.

The theory works as follows:

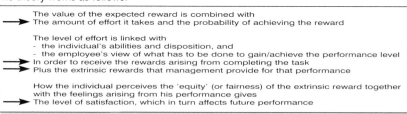

The value of the expected reward is combined with
The amount of effort it takes and the probability of achieving the reward

The level of effort is linked with
- the individual's abilities and disposition, and
- the employee's view of what has to be done to gain/achieve the performance level
In order to receive the rewards arising from completing the task
Plus the extrinsic rewards that management provide for that performance

How the individual perceives the 'equity' (or fairness) of the extrinsic reward together with the feelings arising from his performance gives
The level of satisfaction, which in turn affects future performance

This can be shown diagrammatically thus:

PROCESS THEORY

EXPECTANT MAN

MODEL FOR LAWLER'S THEORY

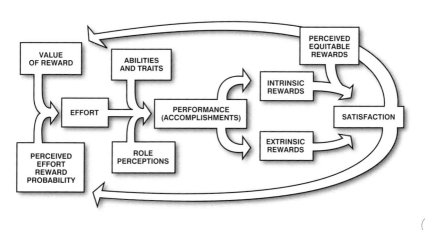

PROCESS THEORY

EXPECTANT MAN

MANAGEMENT TIPS

- Ensure you know what rewards your subordinates value
  - Rewards must match individual needs
  - Recognise that people are different in their requirements

- Decide on the performance level you require
  - If you don't know what you want you cannot communicate it to your employees

- Performance must be possible
  - If the target is too high employees will not try
  - Where possible and appropriate employees should participate in setting the standards required

- Performance must always be linked to the same rewards so that employees know there is a firm link between the two

- The size of the reward must match the proportion of effort, and be perceived as fair and worth the effort

DISPOSITIONAL THEORIES:
TYPES, DISPOSITION & PERSONALITY

DIFFERENT STROKES

Apart from formal theories, another way of thinking about motivation is to think about individuals, their differences and what might motivate them.

The difficulty with any particular theory is that it is supposed to work with everyone on a 'one size fits all' approach. Whilst there are some general rules which apply to everyone, most people are usually motivated **by what they perceive as rewards**. By and large, it is 'different strokes for different folks' to get them committed and motivated.

Obviously, there are going to be overlaps with the various theories covered so far but in this section we take a more individualistic view.

We examine two major approaches:

People Types

and

Dispositional Types

ACHIEVEMENT MAN

McCLELLAND'S THEORY

This theory suggests that at work employees have three needs:

- Achievement
- Power
- Affection

and, according to their personality, one of these needs will dominate the individual.

ACHIEVEMENT MAN

The need for achievement (n-Ach)

This is the desire to take personal responsibility for resolving a problem and seeing a job or task through to completion. Thus, the individual gains a personal feeling of accomplishment from his or her success.

People with high **n-Ach** tend to set themselves goals which, although stretching, have a high possibility of success.

It is essential for these people to have feedback on their performance. They must know how well they are doing.

ACHIEVEMENT MAN

The need for power (n-Power)

This is the desire to control and influence others. It is a real need to be in charge of others, irrespective of the situation. Such people will be hard so that they can obtain positions of influence and power over others.

The need for affection (n-Aff)

This is the desire to be liked and respected by others. It is the need to be wanted and recognised by others for who you are, what you do and the contribution you make.

Research suggests that effective managers are higher on **n-Ach** and **n-Power** than on **n-Aff**.

SELF-LIMITING MAN

SELF-CONFIDENCE THEORY

"If you think you can or if you think you can't, you're right", said Henry Ford and, in so doing, captured the essence of this theory.

Many people are self-limiting in their views about their own ability and capacities. They have the mind-sets 'I can't do that' and, consequently, they either fail or don't even try in the first place.

When Roger Bannister first broke that impossible target of the four-minute mile, three other people did the same within the following 12 months and now there are hundreds of sub-four-minute milers. Bannister, by doing it first, broke not only a time barrier but also a psychological barrier, thus encouraging other athletes to think they could do the same.

To motivate people, a manager's job is to encourage people to be positive about themselves and believe in what they can do, so that they will challenge what they previously thought impossible.

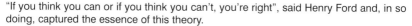

SELF-LIMITING MAN

MANAGEMENT TIPS

- Set targets that stretch employees
- Encourage employees to believe in themselves
- Reward employees for trying, as well as for successful performance

Remember, employees can only succeed in the targets that they believe they can achieve.

TYPES, DISPOSITION & PERSONALITY

FAIR MAN

EQUITY THEORY

We do not work in isolation and being aware of what others do and how they are rewarded has an effect on our motivation. We compare what we get with what others receive. We also compare how hard we work with the amount of effort others put in. We balance this information to see if the rewards/effort relationship is fair, thus creating a rough and ready formula that looks something like this:

$$\frac{\textbf{My Remuneration}}{\textbf{My Effort}} \quad \textbf{Should Match} \quad \frac{\textbf{Your Remuneration}}{\textbf{Your Effort}}$$

FAIR MAN

EQUITY THEORY

J. Stacy Adams originally developed this theory, and called it Equity Theory. When we make the comparisons and feel that we come off worse, we perceive our situation as lacking in equity. Not only do we feel frustrated but our motivation is affected. We may respond in one of several ways:

- Reduce our input (effort) until the rewards are seen as fair, ie: decrease motivation
- Do what we can to increase our rewards or our remuneration, ie: increase motivation

If this is not possible we might even resolve our frustration by leaving the organisation.

Sometimes people will distort their view of their own or others' performance to achieve fairness. If you are doing well in the equation you tell yourself that it is because you work harder, or are more experienced, or have more responsibilities than the person to whom you are comparing yourself. Alternatively, if you perceive them as better off you may think that their work is not as enjoyable or as interesting as yours, or that their family life suffers.

FAIR MAN
MANAGEMENT TIPS

- Recognise that people will make comparisons about job and remuneration levels
- Identify areas where employees will have knowledge of pay levels
- Ensure bonuses match perceptions about effort, experience, responsibilities, etc
- Ensure that job titles, spans of control, budget authority, etc, are comparable one with another, and form sensible levels of differentials, that are perceived to be fair

GAMBLING MAN
VALENCE THEORY

Man is a gambling animal. We make choices and take risks from the options that are available to us. We will choose the behaviour which we think will give us the best outcome and deliver what we want. This theory allows for conscious decision-making by the employee.

The elements of the theory are:

- Outcome — What is possible as a result of behaviour

- Valence — How desirable or attractive is the outcome

- Expectancy — The perceived relationship between the behaviour and the outcome, ie: 'If I do this will I get that?'

Thus the formula is:
Behaviour = Expectancy + Valence

(71)

GOOD MAN/BAD MAN

THEORY X & Y

This theory is based upon your management attitude towards your employees. According to Douglas McGregor, you are either a Theory X or a Theory Y manager and your outlook will influence the way you attempt to motivate your employees.

If you are a Theory **X** Manager then you believe that your employees:

- Hate working
- Dislike responsibility
- Have minimum ambition
- Have no ideas
- Cannot solve difficulties
- Only work for the money
- Need total control
- Are lazy and not to be trusted

TYPES, DISPOSITION & PERSONALITY

GOOD MAN/BAD MAN

THEORY X

So if you are a Theory **X** Manager you believe that the only way to motivate your employees is to:

- Tell them exactly: what to do
  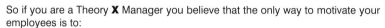
  when to do it
  how to do it
- Provide close supervision
- Make all the decisions yourself
- Allow no participation
- Give rewards only in pay
- Expect minimum contribution

Sadly, and strange as it might seem, this is still the prevailing management style used in most enterprises today. Employees are expected to be placid and give little except the specific labour they are contracted to give.

GOOD MAN/BAD MAN

THEORY Y

If you are a Theory **Y** Manager then you believe that your employees:

- Enjoy their work
- Want to make a contribution
- Willingly accept responsibility
- Can make decisions for themselves
- Are able to solve problems
- Are able to make long term plans and achieve them

GOOD MAN/BAD MAN

THEORY Y

If you are a Theory **Y** Manager you believe that to motivate your employees you:

- Give them responsibility
- Let them make decisions about their work
- Let them make and implement suggestions
- Reward them in other ways than just money

Most employees are good citizens, pay their taxes, educate and raise their children well, aspire to and work hard for the good things in life. They do not lose these aspirations, skills and abilities when they come to work.

The wise manager (the Theory **Y** Manager) will harness all this potential and, in so doing, increase the productivity of those being managed.

GOOD MAN/BAD MAN

THEORY Y MANAGEMENT TIPS

- Involve employees as much as possible in as many decisions that affect them as possible
- Invite, recognise and reward comments, suggestions and ideas
- Reward individual and group initiative and those who take responsibility
- Facilitate group discussion and decision-making
- Develop trust and respect for employees
- Encourage employees to develop themselves and their skills so that they may reach their maximum potential

PEOPLE TYPES

It is obvious that from time to time different things will appeal to us. In this section we look at the different types of people - using as a basis Maslow's hierarchy of needs and McClelland's work - and see how different approaches might motivate different types of people.

The categories we shall review will be as follows:

- Security and comfort
- Affiliation and friendship
- Organisation and structure
- Status and authority
- Individuality and autonomy

TYPES, DISPOSITION & PERSONALITY

SECURITY & COMFORT

As we know from Maslow, security is one of the most basic of all motivators. However, there are individuals who are drawn to this need more keenly than others. This is usually because of some serious deprivation at a significant period in their life.

Those likely to seek security and comfort will be those who:

- Went without when they were young
- Augmented family income at an early age
- Take promotions or change positions mainly to increase just the income component of their job
- Like to show off their wealth

Such people will be motivated by:
- Perceived high income
- Bonus payments
- Predictable long term benefits

In fact, these people will be rewarded by all the hygiene factors!

TYPES, DISPOSITION & PERSONALITY

AFFILIATION & FRIENDSHIP

This is the need to be liked and accepted by others, to have friends and to have places to go (as the song says) where 'everyone knows your name'.

Those likely to seek affiliation and friendship will be those who:
● Come from large families and tend to be the younger members of the family
● Have long-lasting friendships
● Seek out social situations during their spare time
● More likely to be women than men

Those people will be motivated by:
● The encouragement of social relationships at work
● Team working arrangements
● Opportunities to talk and share at work
● Jobs where there is mutual dependence upon one another
● Opportunities to care for or give service to others

Interestingly enough, this type of person is not usually interested in running things or being in charge, nor do they aspire to senior management positions.

ORGANISATION & STRUCTURE

This approach is close to the need for security and comfort. Its difference lies in the fact that people find comfort in belonging to any identifiable group. Whilst it might appear like a social need, it is not quite the same, but rather a requirement for regulation, predictability and structure in one's life.

Those likely to seek organisation and structure will be those who:
- Had an unsettled early childhood
- Had a very structured upbringing
- Had parents who enjoyed secure life-long employment
- Change jobs very infrequently
- Have been unexpectedly retrenched
- Enjoy working to rules and regulations in a predictable working environment

These people will be motivated by:
- Set goals and procedures
- Firm rules and regulations
- Predictable work outcomes
- Long term pension and benefits
- Promotion based upon seniority
- Work which has few surprises

STATUS & AUTHORITY

This is the need to have power and influence over others; to be able to control and direct the behaviour of subordinates or peers.

Those likely to seek status and authority will be those who:

- Are first-born
- Gravitated to power positions at school or college
- Organise things in their spare time
- Put themselves forward to be elected in social groups
- Enjoyed supervisory or managerial responsibility at an early age
- Are dominant in relationships

These people will be motivated by opportunities to:

- Lead
- Direct and control
- Take charge
- Persuade and influence
- Achieve goals and targets
- Compete

INDIVIDUALITY & AUTONOMY

This is when people feel the need 'to do it their way'; where self-fulfilment and independence are important aspects of their lives. They are more interested in self-control than the control of others.

Those likely to seek individuality and autonomy will be those who:

- Have a strong need to be creative
- Like to be personally challenged
- Place an emphasis on lifestyle
- Have difficulty with structure and predictability
- Take personal responsibility for growth
- Have high expectations of self

These people will be motivated by:

- Personal goals and targets
- Opportunities to learn and develop
- Opportunities to be creative
- Opportunities to solve problems and find solutions
- Opportunities to do new things

DISPOSITION & MOTIVATION

This suggests that if you can recognise the disposition or personality of the person, then you can motivate them accordingly, since different people value different things.

In the following taxonomy it is suggested that there are four different and distinct personality types.

Of course, there are far more than four personality types, indeed there are as many types as there are individuals, but this helps us attempt different motivational approaches with different people.

- Helpful people
- Directive people
- Consolidative people
- Adaptive people

Each of these responds differently to motivational opportunities.

With a little bit of thought it is possible for a manager to place a subordinate in one of the four types and then work with that person in the way that makes him or her feel most comfortable - thus more motivated.

HELPFUL PEOPLE

Helpful people are those who are:

- Thoughtful
- Idealistic
- Modest
- Trusting

- Loyal
- Receptive
- Co-operative

Helpful people will be motivated by:

- Worthwhile causes
- Idealistic appeals

- Requests for help
- Emphasis on self-development

In work environments which are:

- Respectful
- Supportive

- Reassuring
- Idealistic

DIRECTIVE PEOPLE

Directive people are those who are:

- Controlling
- Quick to act
- Self-confident
- Persuasive
- Competitive
- Risk-taking
- Urgent

Directive people will be motivated by:

- Opportunity
- Responsibility
- Challenges
- Authority
- Power and status

In work environments which are:

- Competitive
- Direct
- Risk orientated
- Opportunistic

CONSOLIDATIVE PEOPLE

Consolidative people are those who are:

- Tenacious
- Steadfast
- Practical
- Thorough
- Economical
- Methodical
- Reserved
- Detail orientated
- Factual
- Analytical

Consolidative people will be motivated by:

- Facts and figures
- Tangible outcomes
- Approaches
- Analysis
- Practical work

In work environments which are:

- Detail orientated
- Fair
- Systematic
- Consistent
- Objective
- Structured

ADAPTIVE PEOPLE

Adaptive people are those who are:

- Flexible
- Experimenting
- Youthful
- Enthusiastic
- Tactful

- Adaptable
- Socially skilful
- Animated
- Inspiring

Adaptive people will be motivated by:

- Opportunities to shine
- Highly social environments
- High variety

- Change
- Opportunities to grow and learn

In work environments which are:

- Friendly
- Fun
- Sociable

- Understanding
- Expansive

- Optimistic
- Rule free

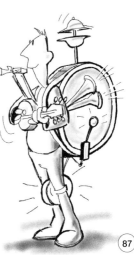

87

NOTES

MOTIVATING INDIVIDUALS AT WORK

MOTIVATING WORDS

Given that we are influenced and persuaded to purchase goods and services through advertising, then we would be wise to be aware of the most frequently used words that bombard us daily from billboards, TV, newspapers and journals. If these words work on us then maybe we can use them on others to persuade them.

Apparently the most popular words used are:

Good   **Guaranteed**   SAFE

MONEY   *Love*   **FREE**   **Discover**

Health   *Own*   **New**   **Best**

Proven   Results

So, when motivating people, we should, where appropriate, practise using these words as much as possible in our management instructions.

WHAT EMPLOYEES WANT

If we wish to motivate employees we need to understand what they want from work. Most employers treat employees as if only pay is important (Theory X) but, as demonstrated by most of the theories outlined in this book, this is not the most significant requirement in a job.

In a very large study researchers asked employers to rank in order (most important first) what they thought employees wanted from their jobs. Then they asked employees what they wanted, again in rank order. There was a significant difference in the results, shown below:

Aspect of work	Employers' rank	Employees' rank
Good wages	1	5
Job security	2	4
Promotions	3	7
Good working conditions	4	9
Interesting work	5	6
Management loyalty	6	8
Fair discipline	7	10
Appreciation	8	1
Help on personal problems	9	3
Feeling involved	10	2

WHAT EMPLOYEES WANT

Employees want the following:

- Appreciation
- Feeling involved
- Help with personal problems

In fact, those aspects of work that recognise employees as real people who have individual feelings and aspirations. This links in with the higher needs of Maslow's theory (Pyramid Man) and the 'satisfiers' of Herzberg's growth theory (Growth Man).

The implication is that whilst employers thought employees wanted more than anything
1. Good wages   2. Job security   3. Promotions
these are not the things that motivate and interest employees most.

The management tips are now obvious:
- Show as much appreciation for good work as possible
- Involve your subordinates in as many work decisions as possible
- Show real care and help for employees in difficulty or with problems

THE SPORTS COACH APPROACH

Athletes go to phenomenal lengths to be successful at what they do. To be successful, not only do they have to be physically fit, they must also be motivated and have the right mind-set. The list that follows is an amalgam of what coaches of international athletes do to motivate their protégés. You can see how closely their actions follow formal motivational theories.

- Regular use of praise and encouragement
- Individual rewards contingent on performance
- Rewards given as soon after success as possible
- Rewards and praise given sincerely, enthusiastically and repeatedly
- Encouragement of others (team members, friends, colleagues) to give praise for good performance
- Rewards not only for winning but also for personal bests and 'giving of the best'
- Encouragement of athletes to reward themselves with what they value as significant for them

COME ON!
COME ON!

KEEPING YOURSELF MOTIVATED

As a manager you have to be motivated yourself in order to motivate others. Now you know the theory you can begin to apply it to yourself.

1	Regularly review what you have achieved each day, month and year; set SMART goals for yourself.
2	Develop a personal reward system for small, medium, large and milestone successes; contract with yourself that you will always give of your best.
3	Regularly review your personal goals and targets; go for everything you can.
4	Develop a mental picture of yourself doing and achieving what you aspire to; give everything you do total focus.
5	Keep a success file and record all your achievements; rejoice and celebrate success; keep learning from your experience (your successes as well as your failures).
6	Look after your health by eating, resting and exercising appropriately; look after your body so that you are fit, alert and healthy.
7	Ensure that your self-talk is positive; continually visualise success.
8	Keep a confidence file, a list of everything you like and admire about yourself.
9	Use positive affirmations and say them to yourself regularly.
10	Avoid making comparisons with others.

CONFIDENCE ACTIVITY

Sometimes it is difficult to motivate yourself. Thinking about what you are good at and what you have achieved builds confidence, and confidence helps you motivate yourself. If you are motivated you can motivate others.

1 My greatest achievement is..

2 Something I am good at is ....

3 I have helped others by ....

4 The best decision I ever made was ....

5 If I want I can ....

6 People think I'm good at ....

7 Something I have learnt to do recently is ....

8 Something I am proud of is ....

9 My proudest moment has been ....

10 The most difficult thing I ever did was ....

MOTIVATING INDIVIDUALS AT WORK

100 WAYS OF SAYING WELL DONE

1. That's great
2. Good job
3. Excellent
4. I appreciate that
5. That's looking good
6. Good work
7. Great work
8. You're doing well
9. Good to have you on the team
10. You made the difference
11. Exceptional
12. Thanks for the extra
13. Wonderful
14. That is so significant
15. Superb
16. Perfect
17. Just what was needed

18. Centre button
19. A significant contribution
20. Wow
21. Fantastic
22. Thank you
23. Just what the doctor ordered
24. First class
25. Nice job
26. Way to go
27. Far out
28. Just the ticket
29. You are a legend
30. Very professional
31. Where would we be without you
32. Brilliant
33. Top marks

34. Impressive
35. You hit the target
36. Neat
37. Cool
38. Bullseye
39. How did you get so good
40. Beautiful
41. Just what was wanted
42. Impressive
43. Great
44. Just right
45. Congratulations
46. Very skilled
47. I'm glad you're on my team
48. It is good to work with you
49. You did us proud
50. This is going to make us shine

100 WAYS OF SAYING WELL DONE

51. Well done
52. I just love it
53. You are fantastic
54. Great job
55. Professional as usual
56. You take the biscuit every time
57. I'm proud of you
58. Don't ever leave us
59. Are you good or what?
60. The stuff of champions
61. Cracking job
62. First class job
63. Magnificent
64. Bravo
65. Amazing
66. Simply superb
67. Triple 'A'

68. Perfection
69. Poetry in motion
70. Sheer class
71. World class
72. Polished performance
73. Class act
74. Unbelievable
75. Gold plated
76. Just classic
77. Super
78. Now you're cooking
79. You are so good
80. You deserve a pat on the back
81. Tremendous job
82. Unreal
83. Treasure
84. Crash hot

85. You beauty
86. The cat's meow
87. I just can't thank you enough
88. You always amaze me
89. Magic
90. Another miracle
91. Terrific
92. What a star
93. Colossal
94. Wonderful
95. Top form
96. You're one of a kind
97. Unique
98. Way out
99. Incredible
100. Ace

THE NINE RULES OF MOTIVATION

1   You must be motivated to motivate.

2   Motivation requires a SMART Goal.

3   Motivation, once established, does not last forever.

4   Motivation requires lots of individual recognition.

5   To motivate you must participate.

6   Progress and success motivates.

7   Challenge only motivates if you can succeed.

8   We all have motivational hot buttons.

9   Team membership motivates.

About the Author

Max A. Eggert BSc, MA, FCIPD, CFAHRI, ABPS, MAPS
Max is a management psychologist specialising in assisting individuals reach their
maximum potential. Besides being retained by major international corporations as
coach, mentor and strategist, he has been interviewed frequently on TV, radio and
in the print media both in Australia and in Europe. His work and publications have
been reviewed both in the professional journals and the specialist media.
He has also lectured at premier universities as well as leading many professional
conferences.

Max has degrees in psychology, industrial relations and theology. He has fifteen books in print in
twelve languages, one of which is a standard text and two are frequently in the ten best business
books. Several of his books are on the recommended reading lists of Sydney, London, Harvard,
Westminster and Sussex Universities. In the Pocketbook Series he has also written: The Assertiveness
Pocketbook, The Managing Your Appraisal Pocketbook and The Resolving Conflict Pocketbook.

Contact
Transcareer Pty Ltd
Level 31
88 Phillip Street
Sydney
NSW 2000
AUSTRALIA

Tel: +61 2 8211 0500
Fax: +61 2 8211 0555
Mobile: 040 360 2286
Email: max@transcareer.com.au

> "Max is an international
> psychologist who has the gift of
> making the complexities of human behaviour
> understandable and relevant to business."
> **Financial Times, London**

ORDER FORM

Your details

Name _____

Position _____

Company _____

Address _____

_____

Telephone _____

Fax _____

E-mail _____

VAT No. (EC companies) _____

Your Order Ref _____

Please send me:

No. copies

The <u>Motivation</u> Pocketbook ☐

The _____ Pocketbook ☐

The _____ Pocketbook ☐

The _____ Pocketbook ☐

The _____ Pocketbook ☐

Order by Post

MANAGEMENT POCKETBOOKS LTD

LAUREL HOUSE, STATION APPROACH,
ALRESFORD, HAMPSHIRE SO24 9JH UK

Order by Phone, Fax or Internet

Telephone: +44 (0)1962 735573
Facsimile: +44 (0)1962 733637
E-mail: sales@pocketbook.co.uk
Web: www.pocketbook.co.uk

MANAGEMENT POCKETBOOKS